MYSTIQUE OF THE WILY TROUBADOUR

METAPHORS OF THE ABSURD

DEBABRATA ROY

Dedicated to the fond memory of my dear Brother in law, late Dr Subodh Chandra Sinha, Professor Emiritus, University of Manipur, Ethno-botanist, Ecologist, Philanthrope, Social Scientist of International repute, Authority on Medicinal flora of Manipur, honored as one of 'Asia's Who & Who' (seen here with the variety of 'Seroy Lily' he discovered)

Dr Subodh Chandra Sinha

Contents

Contents

Contents

Contents

Foreword

The Mystique of the Wily Troubadour: The Magic of Words

The world-famous poet William Wordsworth rightly said that poetry is the spontaneous overflow of powerful feelings. But when we express something in poetry some inflexible critics may suspect the metrical constraints in it. The spontaneity can't be maintained in the name of grammar and metrics of poetry. The great Sanskrit critic Panditraaj Jagannath had already said in the 17th century AD that poetry is that word that produces beautiful meaning. The romantic poet Percy Bysshe Shelley also opines the same thing in simple words. He says that poetry is the record of the best and happiest moments of the happiest and best minds. In other words, a happy mind only can create some happy moments. But simultaneously, one element is equally important in poetry. For whom we write poems? Who are the readers? Are the readers qualified? The famous Urdu poet Allama Iqbal does not recommend poetry to everyone. He says that poetry is not for idiots. It is only for soft-hearted people. But the ultimate thing in poetry, as Mathew Arnold said, is simply the most beautiful, impressive, and widely effective mode of saying things. Dr. Debabrata Roy is a modern poet who also writes beautiful poems in a beautiful way.

As far as the poetry of Dr. Roy is concerned, as inscribed in the collection The Mystique of the Wily Troubadour, these are no novice's; in the selection of his words and their purported application clearly bear evidence of his solid linguistic and academic background. Poignantly, it was his father who had laid the foundation of poetry in him, and worthy to mention here his scholarly aesthete father was a student at the University of Calcutta and was schooled by towering personalities like none other than Dr. S Radhakrishnan.

Giving birth to a poem is just like giving birth to a baby. The author and the mother have to undergo the same degree of pain while delivering the babies. Someone had asked the famous Hindi poet, Dr. Harivansrai Bachchan, "What is your masterpiece?" Then Dr. Bachchan replied, "I have two masterpieces—one is *Madhushala* and the other is *Amitabh*. In other words, every creation by a poet is equally dear to him. All of Dr.Roy's poems are beautiful and are built on subtle & beautiful nuances of thoughts. I was already a fan of Dr. Roy and now I have become a fan of his poetry also. Here I am tempted to quote a few lines from his poem *Facade* that exemplifies his emotional intelligence & dexterity with words:

> *this ornate facade*
> *of calculated homily*
> *is ruthless!*
> *robs the autumn sky its signature azure*
> *the moon its stately charm*
> *gold lacquered morning its glee*
> *and we know it!*
> *need to set them free—*
> *the primordial and profound in everlasting bliss*
> *the dance and the danseuse*
> *the flame and the luminescence!*

Lastly, I would say that Dr. Roy has beautifully challenged some stereotypes while composing his poems. He has taken 'artistic liberty' to not capitalize the initial words in the lines of any of his poems. I would not like to make any comment on this. I would rather quote few lines of famous Urdu poet Javed Akhtar for the poet here:

> *Jidhar jate hain sab jana udhar achchha nahin lagta,*
> *Mujhe paamaal raste ka safar achchha nahin lagta,*
> *Mujhe dushman se bhi khuddari ki ummeed rahti hai*
> *Kisi ka bhi ho sar qadmon men sar achchha nahin lagta!*

- Pramod Bharatiya, M.A., MPhil, Ph.D., D. Litt
Postgraduate College Mussorie, Dehradun, UK,IND

Acknowledgements

I am humbled at the loving & proactive insistence of and gratefully acknowledge the kindred souls who wished & made this anthology happen.

I am morally obliged to mention a man of rare wisdom and a votary of truth- of whom I am previleged to be begotten, my dear late father, Shri Hemendra Chandra Roy, an academician philanthrope of unsurpassed eminence, erudition & enigma who in his inimitable, quiet resolve- firm yet affectionate- molded & mentored me, exhorted me to listen, perceive, learn & imagine too

Professor Emiritus, Dr Subodh Chandra Sinha, my late brother-in-law comes immediately to mind, who sincerely believed (and made me shudder) I was meant to do great things in life! Needless to say, barely have I lived upto his conviction. I dedicate this anthology to him who loved me like his own child.

I feel extremely privileged & thankful to acclaimed scholar, author, literateur & asthete of repute Dr Promod Bhartiya who kindly wrote a prologue to the compilation.

I can not thank enough the bright & brilliant Dr Yashendra Sethi, my dear student of many parts & promise who almost singlehandedly bore the mantle of this publication process.

I must gratefully speak of versatile Dr Desh Deepak, colleague & friend and Dr Vidisha, Dr Richa, Dr Ravleen, Dr Uttamjyot- all my students who took pains to read stuff I wrote and even sincerely found these good too!

And of course, heartfelt love & thanks to my family- Dr Leena (wife), Ruben & Ivan (sons), Buri (niece) who indulgently & patiently bore with me through the sojourn

Signing off, feel impelled to acknowledge the timeless tryst with the 'muse', ethereal & elusive, whom my eager, desperate words have continued to seek...

Prologue

Mine has been an imminently intimate engagement of random soliloquy, of visualizing metaphors, of imageries- improbable & the absurd- and these morphing into many hued scape of otherwise unassuming words with a recurring refrain that one may hardly miss while kindly bearing with the liberty I dared take- by all means more than & unlike any 'artistic' kind.

One would rather I brandished wordstrokes to enframe that sly 'thought-fox' (as Ted Hughes'd say) into a word- mural, a fresco or say, I chiseled & sculpted intaglios in maverick wordsmithy.... why, even wordmongering!

Let me confess escapades of such kind remained a sacred secret only I would make forays into and embers of which I only stoked at times unbeknown to others but for a few trusted ones.

Also, it will be too conspicuous not to strike a discerning reader the liberty I took in not following any particular idiom defining poetry.I wanted these unfettered, happily unbound if not unbridled.

1. Hymns

teeming silence
occult & pre-historic
(of the Galapagos, Samoa or Tahiti as it were)
of many an epic tale
and many a springtide
bled and froze into viscid grey hymns-
stunning macabre monoliths
these hymns
yet mere constructs we lived & named
and knew won't ever thaw or singe.

2. Trust me please

trust me
for the umpteenth time
the demure jacaranda shall break into a sprightly rustle
bid good riddance to the very profligate northerly
and the ever itinerant geese
shall call it time
to the exotic grassland
(they had fondly nested a while)
and wing back to the velvet silence of the Tundra-
trust me
for the umpteenth time
the magic spring-tide
awash in soft olive sun-shine,
(a 'nymphet' in slovenly pubescence as it were)
that had mesmerized & stunned us
(as the 'prurient southern wind blew ever so gently over our garden')
and withered unsung
warped forever into ' intaglio- moments'
light-years away...
shall verily come alive
and play out that ubiquitous chiaroscuro
for the umpteenth time
trust me
the gaze, intense & feral
that had set a preternatural twilight afire
stalked the unassuming pine-wood,

(along the serpentine NH 39 you know)
and could bring many a knight to their knees with ruthless ease
& shall come alive for the umpteenth time!

• 3 •

3. Bliss

the golden oriole
bucolic dreams in its kohl eyes
green warmth
of polynesian islands under its wings
and wily petunias
connive & revel
in a riot of colored glee
springtide wells up
and sapphire tongues of bliss
light a sweet consumption afire!

4. At dusk

and soon enough
dusk shall cascade down the valley
an ebony nymphet
serenading like a danseuse
the soliciting night into the sacred alcove
and last of the ravens winging its way
into the twilight just the way it has been forever
weary souls gaze at a faraway wonderland
feign bonhomie & hubris
miserable deluded souls preserving pathetic selves
on ephemeral coordinates
weaving tender bleeding yarns of happiness !
a scheming wench-
for a tomorrow that never
ever comes

5. Insolent Words

sifting through a shoal of words
or rather a drove of them
I'd harvest some-
not the unweildy insolent ones
(street-smart & roughened with callosities)
rather
the soft malleable & ductile ones-
those I can browbeat into submission!
so I may set them to do my bidding
and embody those imminently fleeting
moments of revelation of unsurpassed brilliance
I'd drape & bejewel these cohorts of docile words
at once intense & tender
into metaphorical vessels
of an elysian engagement!

6. Unassuming words

unassuming words

inert & austere

morph into mysterious dynamic

of sheer texture & contour

as in a Boticelli venus-

of dreams......

and as intense & electric

as Gaugin's sacred murals-

bind in gleeful chimeric spell

of soulful implosion!

sly hedonism

this voyeuristic retreat;

from rigmarole

of paranoid self preservation

into vain quixotic wordsmithy

at miserable expense

of unassuming words

inert & austere !

7. Of metaphors

metaphors have ceased to be game
like I could get them eat out of my hands
at will (you know)
as it 'd rain relentless & inane
I can only think of the wily troubadour
and his tambourine
bugyals and conifer groves in stupor
and say, a pining smitten mountain lass etc
or may be I might just hear
a wailing restive boat-woman
a voluptuous Titas intently listening to her dirge
why even demure oleander, coy hibiscus, petite jasmine
& inebriated thick air
the ubiquitous wet crow
and of course, impossible forays into the mysterious
into irresistible mythical wilderness...
metaphors have ceased to be game!

8. And then again

And then again
wintering stilts and pintails too
dreaming of a celtic twilight
shall call time
on a beige morning,
wing their way home
across seven seas & four winds
and tell amazing stories...
of exotic savannah &
riverine rain-forests
of pining lonely women
at star-lit mountain hamlets
of wizened oak grove
& starry eyed great bear
maimed restive conifers ,
of emerald silence
gravid with sacred rites of passage...
why even shreik into livid pulsatile bits of mirth
our maudlin secrets and set us free

9. Just as well

let's say
an immaculate incubus in repose
at the ocean's womb
we, woke up at the wondrous alternate sky-
an emerald twilight of oblivion
in exile we froze in fear
we trod lonely paths in wilderness
many a mistral we weathered
in trepidation we met
and preserved our pathetic forlorn selves
it hasn't been easy
but that's just as well

10. Silent soprano

ingots of molten gold
bejewel this december morning
a nymphet in pubescence
a high-land lass as it were
her chandelier laughter broke
into sparkling smithereens
her song a silent cascading soprano
we had rather reconcile
to this primeval fount of mirth
this magic morning
of filial glee welling up
in benign acceptance
this quiet implosion too
and this exalted awareness
of an immaculate consumption
of a zillion tongues of lapis lazuli fire
of bliss-
we had rather reconcile

11. Calculated homily

'let's talk of the weather'
or not talk at all
this ornate facade of calculated homily
is ruthless
robs the autumn sky its signature azure
the moon its stately charm
gold lacquered morning its glee
and we know it!
as hours break like surf in impetuous monotone
whipped out of all senses
oh! the benign solitude is merely skin-deep
and silence festers like a wound
'let's talk of the weather'
or not talk at all

12. Winged heartaches

a saturnine impasse
incubates tender reservoir of pain
singe & hold at ransom
the mute conifers
viscid darkness they drink
and turns blue insidiously
and the night primordial & profound lumbers along
a behemoth-
winged heartaches ricochet off it
inane & trivia as it were, these;
the pine wood sulks
a saturnine impasse
incubates tender reservoir of pain

13. Hiatus

this hiatus looms innocuous
like a lull
a predicament-
is in fact a dreary uncharted void
of myriad faceless possibilities
it inspires awe, it frightens
even the ever loyal & trusted words
play truant!
this unfolding of purpose
of my very own space & time
inevitable & ordained, this bidding of the great Leviathan!
shall carry my own stake though
trudge along 'the bridge across forever'
and the world a lorn wench meanwhile
implores & serenades to be mine

14. It's not often

it's not often
one gets to inhabit the elysian space
between gripping tales
told over a thousand arcadian nights
that four winds & seven seas
dare not trespass!
it's not often
you witness irridiscent tongues
of a teeming primordium
and listen to an emerald silence
brew & shreik into rippling peals
across zillion light years
that everything was
just happenstance, that it was all written
that it was a sojourn into myriad worlds
and that we got to bear our
very own stakes

15. A Chekov's evening

iridescent moon- flakes fell in glee
peals of silver laughter in allegretto, these;
drove the deepening dusk & the cedar grove
into a trance
and the breeze philandered with the nubile evening's apparel
a Titian's chiaroscuro played in the rosewood thicket
a quintessential 'Chekov's' evening it was
(wasn't it the sullen Dimov from 'the grasshopper' I met?)
or, maybe, Eliott's evening of 'the wasteland' it was-
where beautiful women came & went
but certainly not talking of Michelangelo!

16. An witness

philia or eros
mirth or melancholia-
very predictable & relentless soiree, this;
inane with a riverine monotone
quite unlike the wanton springtide we knew!
one'd rather it's a beige pastiche,
(say) a post harvest mien of the listless & lorn earth
and lost, weary visages from improbable coordinates
dot light years-
the kohl black lagoon, winding dusty road
coy hibiscus, the solitary crow
the phlegmatic moon and of course
the smitten highland lass...
we'd rather witness these
with unwavering integrity and betray nothing!

17. Metaphorical vessels

18. At the appointed time

it's certain
at the appointed time
we'd stop playing maudlin cameos
and cassandra crossed feral wind'd
cease to blow
coven of visages that hold us hostage
would just disappear
and instead
benediction the color of the nest
of a wintering raven
and a philia
the warmth of a turquoise lagoon
would suffuse the firmament
and drive it to a thrall!

thus anointed
we'd vindicate a prophesy-
at the appointed time!

19. Rembrandt's colts

Rembrandt's colts awash in moonshine
would morph out of the mist and leap
into this serendip soiree
stir and neigh
into thousand pieces
the zircon silence of the wheat fields-
they wouldn't bear to wait you know
they'd prance , preen
and gleefully maul
velvet hearts of the napier;
such were the times-
there aren't any two ways
about the truth
that we'd be willing voyeurs and catch our breath!
trust me

20. Baptism in solitude

travel weary & listless itinerant clouds-
incorrigible, lovelorn damsels- these;
morphed into diaphanous dreams
and spun magic on the smitten cedar & pine wood
they dreamt-
nubile & fecund one day
they'd just pour
their laden hearts out
drench the conifers
the napier, the brown eager earth
into a rhapsody
and an ordained consecration!
this communion was profound
this proximity a sacred covenant-
this baptism in solitude!

21. Comprador muse

it's not easy
to keep holding the four winds
it's not easy either
to raise the bar
or cross the threshold
and witness
comprador muse violate the sacred covenant
we made;
and wallow
in germane endorphins
that assuage
all cowardice & caprice ....

22. Only the journey

There never was any destination
only the journey
just the rhapsody & the thrall
of thousand horsemen in a moor's blood
in the ready, as it were
to take on preternatural mythical beasts
at high seas, intimidating prairie & cold savannah-
a feral glee of conquest
at bringing the elusive peaks & stoic ravines
mysterious pine wood & wily cedars
to their knees...
and of course
the purple angst & pining
the saffron pain of treading on dead sunflower fields
once gravid with stories
but never ever told!
many fell out-
the 'destined' ones
and the wanderer struts along
with a pronounced stoop
the lonely wayfarer!

23. Pilgrimage

bear with me
when I tell you
of the frozen polyphony
that wizened mountains muse
under the watch of a moonstruck seraph;
of the monochrome silence
a primordial incubus
that the soliloquy of a relentless surf
try to break;
trust me please, if you will—
I am not an illusionist
that by mere sleight
shall get unassuming austere words
and draw word-murals of 'inverse reality'!
It's not a quixotic soiree
(trust me)
into exalted ruins
now a babel
(that once was the promised land
'flowing with milk & honey')
it's pilgrimage!

24. There never was...

there wasn't any grander scheme of things
there never was
there wasn't any rubicon to cross
there never was
the syntropy moments we stretched into eternity
the caucus & the polemic
of amazing constructs we so brazenly built

the sleight, the alibi, feigned angst of propriety
we brandished
and of course the veritable peaks we scaled
the eye of the mistral we sat on
the alternate shores we led our voyages to
the immaculate consumption we lit ourselves afire with
the silent riotous implosion
of strangely hued compassion, the benediction
all this & more
we were wont to live, give names and definitions to
and do rites of a mysterious passage...
there wasn't any grander scheme of things
there never was

25. For the umpteenth time...

for the umpteenth time
itinerant fecund geese flew
into beryl warmth of a wondrous solstice
moon-dust on their tired yet resilient wings
their incorrigible hearts
brimming over with a primal philia
the broken earth meanwhile
readied for an immaculate consecration
as usual
for the umpteenth time
and hymns (frozen into monoliths) rose
in mirth at an incredible soprano
the jacaranda (at a thrall and in predicament)
barely hid a rustle in glee
and the Christ's thorn
blushed a livid magenta
for the umpteenth time

a solitary Hsu-Pei-hung's horse stirred
neighed the deepening January mist into shreds
and a stunned pasture woke up
a merry song in tiny hearts of the napier
for the umpteenth time

26. Miasm

wizened frivolous moon & I
reminisce
implausible forays & rendezvous we'd set up
and tip-toe into forbidden ramparts
wearing juvenile, insolent hearts
on our sleeves!
this quixotic self-preservation
like a miasm
grows & feeds itself
on vain rhetoric & rings of denial-
embers of doomed nascent dreams
we so miserably failed to live
yet smoulder
light years away
feel impelled to assuage them!

27. Saffron glee

light-years afire
with coral philia
and sacred preternatural crypts
in a zillion billowing voices muse hosannas
as saffron glee wells up in bosoms
of enamoured geese winging their way
across seven seas relentless
they dare the ruthless north wind
its serrated teeth
their gaze intent & afar
into a verdant land they will nest
their wings searing blue from pain
yet wont to consecrate this ever- lasting tryst
saffron glee wells up in bosoms
of fecund seeds too bursting forth
and nubile stalks as well
dying immaculate deaths into welcome pods
and of course in gravid clouds-
travel weary listless lovelorn damsels,
they dreaming of being nubile one day just pour
their laden hearts & drench the conifers, the napier,
the brown eager earth
and thus consecrate this ever- lasting tryst

28. Baptism in solitude

this communion was profound
this proximity a sacred covenant-
clouds gravid with chamois dreams
hovered over the cedar & pine wood
and the jealous moon witnessed
for the umpteenth time
this baptism in solitude, this smelting-
angels sang hosannas & heavens serenaded
this moment of truth
this baptism in solitude

29. Rippling possibilities

profligate moon
and an effete southern wind
has set up this jeremiad spring evening
you know
jejune thought-foxes sniff die-hard truth
a miserable incubus
cocooned in nebulous rings of denial
that thrive incognito
I need not cross the threshold
and tiptoe into black glory of a 'king-baby'
I have raised the golden bar
I'd rather travel seamlessly
to myriad rippling possibilities
across parallel worlds
forever & at once!

30. Morning-a-Shulamite lass

frivolous spring & its shenanigans
wring her heart
the morning- very nubile and an eager wench
fecund spring has kept her at a thrall
a sprightly gazelle she
canters down the mountains
her flowing tresses auburn & fiery gold
as the charismatic charioteer
whips his magnificent steed
up into the firmament
and nimbly treads on she
beckoning her paramour
a lovelorn Shulamite lass, as it were,
in the cedars of Lebanon'

31. Mysterious passage

there's'nt any grander scheme of things
there never was;
there's'nt any rubicon to cross
there never was;
the syntropy moments we stretched into eternity
the caucus & the polemic
of amazing constructs we so brazenly built
the sleight , the alibi , feigned angst of propriety
we brandished
and of course the veritable peaks we scaled
the eye of the mistral we sat on
the alternate shores we led our voyages to
the immaculate consumption we lit ourselves afire with
the silent riotous implosion of strangely hued compassion
the benediction flowing through veins
all this & more
we were wont to live, give names and definitions to
and do rites of a mysterious passage!
there's'nt any grander scheme of things
there never was

32. Reverie

wintering stilts and pintails
dreaming of a celtic twilight
shall have winged their way home across seven seas
and told amazing stories
of wizened oaks & starry eyed great bear
maimed austere conifers & dreamy mountain hamlets
of meandering streams & rain forests
of lovelorn damsels-
witnesses in an otherworldly seance
of an emerald silence
gravid with a sacred rite of passage
that shrieked into livid pulsatile bits of mirth
and set our maudlin secrets free

33. Autumn requiem

billowing mist, diaphanous & sheer
drapes the hamlet-
a princess lacquered in stardust
and in a sorceress' bind
awaiting that proverbial communion
an autumn requiem-this;
a Renoir or a Van Gokh in tempera!
orphan'd words
like disembodied spirits prowl desolate savannah
of mute longings
and gossamer flakes of purple angst
writhe in an unprecedented ecstacy
I'd rather it is
an ubiquitous Jibanananda,
his deft wordstrokes painting a stunning visual
of a riverine Bengal
its bogs, grasslands in autumnal seance
its bedew'd kans, napier and jasmine
at a thrall!

34. Some other time

some other time

(that died bidden, an orange death into moon-lit bays or beryl twilight)

it'd be a given-

that we'd gleefully look for dark mysterious crypts

into such a silence

(we'd paint it a sombre pastel or ebony, you know)

teeming with an iridescent disquiet

(of myriad wriggling possibilities!)

say, winged sacred hymns

and sepia trails of incorrigible forays

into one too many amazing moments of epiphany

tales of implausible & profound communion

here a laughter, there a sigh

topaz sunshine, piquant rivulets

and a thousand bracing horsemen

their welled up hearts at a bind-

the fiery dragon, the fortress and of course the princess!

that was some other time , some lost coordinate-

words ,no longer eager or prurient

miserably fail to implode

into metaphors of welcome solitude

or engage with an amorphous, barren silence

35. Consecration

dark and sombre

clouds gathered insidious

in feline stealth

over the valley at a lull

and brewed silence

of a strange, intimidating disquiet

itinerant nordic brigands, these

or the moor from exotic shores

(as it were)

their wizened hearts rent asunder

welled up

it rained.

and rained as it did another time

(light-years away you know)

at a bucolic scape

falling on eager myrtle & milkweed

driving them into a thrall;

drenched supple pods of paddy

that burst forth in mirth

frolicked with prurient jute saplings

and cast a spell

on the idyllic jackfruit grove

and a lone wet oriole

the lorn water lily

and the pensive wailing boat-woman

witnessed this profound release

that it was!
a self-effacing rite of passage, this
to glory
to a resurrection
to an ordained consecration
of life!

36. Nimbus & the sapphire consumption

the nimbus
conjured an ebony mystique-
with a swagger and a flourish
of its dark cape
mesmerized the conifers;
brown eager earth
in wanton desire bristled
and held its breath
for a saphire consumption-
an immaculate release!

worn, yellow'd times gave away
layered stucco laid bare
as it were-
familiar quiescent coordinates
across light- years
& alternate shores
in raptures & a thrall !
tender & bleeding coordinates-
of a desperate pubescence,
incorrigible protagonists
and dishonored covenants....

37. Vindication

it's certain
at the appointed time
we'd stop playing maudlin cameos
and cassandra crossed feral wind'd
cease to blow
coven of visages that hold us hostage
would just disappear
and instead
benediction the color of the nest
of a wintering raven and a philia
the warmth of a turquoise lagoon
would suffuse the firmament
and drive it to a stupor
thus anointed
we'd vindicate a prophesy-
at the appointed time!

38. Vain construct

at this vantage

we must condescend

nothing was improbable after all!

'wind from the southern seas would just blow

gently over our garden'

stars light up the path

and we'd have held our tongue

and let us just be!

this anomie

this subservience to sweet lies

this masquerading of ordained truth

held at wilful ransom

in calculated self pity

was s it cowardice exalted

that all propriety forsaken

livid eros feigned seeking filial refuge?

all this merely a surreal vain construct

that truth must set us free!

39. Cryptic call

just so a fabled sorceress
might have brandished her magic wand-
a nebulous cloak of nascent dreams
suffused the evening.
a veiled elusive nymphet
made alive by a sleight one might say
from the lore of Arabian nights
her girdle bells musing a cryptic call
from somewhere at a far away land
light years from now
an abode I belonged to
and yet wandered off

40. Quixotic

star-lit wee hour
in melancholy repose sets in relief
baroque memorabilia
of a travel weary sea-man
gazing at a diaphenous pining mermaid
and mesmerized, walk into a dark & sacred vortex
of the deep blue sea.
memorabilia of wishful quixotic rendezvous
you know
as into the land of alluvial soil, milk and honey
that never'd be his!
for just once more
I might as well feign that sweet trepidation
and tiptoe into that rarefied shore
and gleefully negotiate
rugged contours of passion & despair

41. Ballad from forgotten scrolls

wily balladeer
the sky opened its trove
and crooned
dirges from long forgotten scrolls
of beautiful people
one hadn't time to say a decent good bye
as they fell by the wayside or
disappeared into alternate skies!
rapt conifers listened
to riverine stories of brown coarse rice
smelly dry fish
of pirouetting fakirs
and ghosts on the tamarind tree
the pining boat-woman and of course
maverick tales of restive times
the rains wove
of serendip engagements
with incorrigible pubescence
of passion & pathos
and forbidden forays into the wild!

42. Merry oblivion

chrysalis moments of rainbow passion
die in filial ecstasy
into merry oblivion
the jacaranda grove heaves a sigh
and witness this immaculate communion
the fragrant moistened breeze
wallows at this rite of golden passage
and its heart afire & lorn
whistles a dirge
in silent soprano!....

43. At siege

a zillion light years-
a seamless continuum
by an immaculate sleight
collapsed and froze into a moment!
leviathan one might say humbled into a nadir
of inexorable fecund possibilities
then rising at once and one too many
the spheres mused
a demure pine grove, somnolent hamlets
and the starstruck mountain lass
witness in awe-
as amorphous, inchoate visages
from ossified times
of inordinate fear & bondage
of dreary voyages without ports of call
hold us hostage and at ransom
from owning the truth
that we reneged on the covenant
and let strangers lay siege to our sacred ramparts

44. Of metaphors

metaphors have ceased to be game-
like I could get them eating out of my hands
at will (you know)
as it 'd rain relentless & inane
I can only think of the wily troubadour
and his tambourine,
bugyals and conifer groves in stupor
and say a pining smitten mountain lass...etc
or may be I might just hear
a wailing restive boat-woman-
a voluptuous Titas intently listening to her dirge
why even demure oleander coy hibiscus petite jasmine
& inebriated thick air
the ubiquitous wet crow
and of course impossible forays into the mysterious
into irresistible mythical wilderness
metaphors have ceased to be game!

45. Familiar trappings

just another
of the myriad deepening nights
you know
and all the familiar trappings
so much so it breeds contempt!
an ebony waif
smitten & pensive as usual
and ever itinerant charmers- the delinquent clouds
their hearts on the tether
with a thousand livid tales to tell
(that just can't wait to be told- a mythical release that!)
also the conniving old pedestrian moon
the cedar grove
its mysterious crypts
the renegade muse
and of course the sacrilege
of a mute witness to the plunder
of the promised land
of myrrh aloe & flowing with mil k& honey
all familiar trappings you know
so much so it breeds contempt!

46. Pain

we couldn't pass muster the incipient pain
that stalked & browbeat us-
and therefore ours 've been a relentless engagement
preserving our pathetic selves
we couldn't & won't care any less
and made improbable forays into the dark & the forbidden
we dared the seven seas
and we loved it!
pain has changed its countenance-
doesn't stalk or browbeat anymore
pain now silently implodes into benediction
and humbles
it is'nt easy
to keep holding the four winds
it's not easy either
to raise the bar or cross the threshold
and witness comprador muse violate
the sacred covenant we made
& wallow in germane endorphins
that assuage all cowardice & caprice
lapis lazuli moments waft
under an alabaster swathe
of the wizened moon
and the Orion
as I walk into the vortex of sacred time
and a pining april night fawns

on the terrafirma....
I have a rendezvous light years afar
Tonight!

47. Of thought brigands

mellow colors of senescence
a dollop of yellow here, sepia there
strokes of many hued words
set the winter fresco in comic relief
and betray painfully feigned pubescence
(one might say)
of the proverbial nymphet
from the surreal & implausible shores
(we nested once)
that would've stunned the unassuming jakaranda
we had better
courageously inhabit such intimidating space
of broken covenants, renegade muse
as thought brigands surreptitiously
enticed smitten words, too eager
strokes of many hued words
set the winter fresco in comic relief!

48. Wanton twilight

ambling weary winter-noon
(one would rather)
a pensive lorn wench
imminently feline & primeval
reclined a while at the mountain slope
she seemed to reminisce a thousand solstices
from alternate meridians
and the rapt oak grove won't rustle a leaf!
could it be the story of her avatar-
the smitten waif from the Polynesian isles
of the mysterious south seas,
burgeoning into a wanton twilight?
or her lonesome soirees through mythical grasslands
or say, those wind beaten peccadillos
at the ramparts of Meherangarh fort
and mysterious facades of Noor-e- darwaza?
and ,why it sure could be the account
of her maverick engagements-
her astringent philia with harvest- ready fields
of sprightly paddy and jubilant mustard
of gleaning owls & mice
and of course,
the ubiquitous ghosts on the tamarind tree,
smell of date palm jaggery, dung- cakes,
and vanquished kites sailing away

49. Anomie

at this vantage
we must condescend
nothing was improbable after all!
'wind from the southern seas would just blow
gently over our garden'
stars light up the path
and we'd have held our tongues
and let ourselves just be!
this anomie
this subservience to sweet lies
this masquerading of ordained truth
held at wilful ransom
in calculated self pity-
all this- a surreal vain construct!
truth must set us free

50. Stakes

it's not often
one gets to inhabit the elysian space
between gripping tales
told over a thousand arcadian nights
that four winds & seven seas
dare not trespass!
it's not often
you witness irridiscent tongues
of a teeming primordium
and listen to a onyx silence
billow & shreik into rippling peals
across zillion lightyears
that everything was
just happenstance, that
it was all written, that
it was a sojourn of myriad worlds
and that we got to bear our own stakes

51. Benediction

*this canvas
of a deepening disquiet
notwithstanding,
I shall engage as usual
winged frolicking words;
shall cast, mould & chisel
truant words
eager & supple
and revisit once more
(as a voyeur)
the flaming green angst
feral & intense
of thousand wriggling tongues
of sapphire consumption!
and watch this deepening disquiet
silently retreat
to sheer wordstrokes*

it's benediction....

52. A cameo

sultry dusk
played a cameo
as we put up a veneer
of sanitized pretense
with seasoned ease!
(It was'nt a rendezvous we had set up, you know)
and talked of
weather, cholesterol, inflation.
exchanged pleasantries.....
one could'nt miss
the contour & texture
of now famished & phlegmatic words;
hapless words
in austere submission!
words, once supple, restive & prurient-
and such ones
who could'nt wait to proclaim a truth,
(that once the cosmos connived to uphold!)
how miserably they failed us!
for that matter,
nothing had welled up within
and nothing transpired
so I might use a metaphor!
(say, of a thousand horsemen in the veins raring to strike
or perhaps, an epiphany that the sultry dusk was witness to etc);

and of course
none had braced or bristled
like one did
on a rosy December twilight
by the lakeside
or on a moon -struck spring evening
secretly pining for the wind
from the southern seas...

53. Gambit

this gambit
doesn't work always-
to get them
I mean the words;
seemingly delinquent, prurient children
one might say
to do my bidding
as and when I wish
Even the ones otherwise eager
(whom I would so easily get to eat out of my hands!)
and who couldn't wait, as it were
to seamlessly engage
the encrypted dark Babel
of my mind's hinterland
and emerge aglow
in celebration of beauty & truth-
they too are playing truant & unwieldy!
an intimidating solitude, this.

54. Mien

philia or eros

mirth or melancholia

very predictable & relentless soiree, this;

inane with a riverine monotone

quite unlike

the wanton springtide we knew!

one'd rather

it's a beige post -harvest mien

of the listless & lorn earth

of lost, weary visages from improbable coordinates

dotting light years

the kohl black lagoon, winding dusty road

coy hibiscus, the solitary crow

the phlegmatic moon and of course

the smitten highland lass

we'd rather witness these

with unwavering integrity

and betray nothing!

55. A jeremiad evening

incorrigible moon
and an effete southern wind
has set up a jeremiad spring evening
jejune thought-foxes
sniff die-hard truth- a miserable incubus
cocooned in nebulous rings of denial
that thrive incognito
I need not cross the threshold
and tiptoe into black glory of a 'king-baby';
I have raised the golden bar-
I'd rather travel seamlessly
to myriad rippling possibilities
across parallel worlds
forever & at once!...

56. Deep in December

the northerly
brandishes its serrated cold teeth
and the dark grey mist
like a behemoth from an alternate world
frightens-
the prodigal child makes a serendip soiree
into fear-subterranean & macabre
the hapless child!
revisits improbable forays
into the forbidden
yet ordained engagements
angels would sing hosannas
and the cosmos hold its breath
like mother earth
the muse'd assuage & nurse
the truant child
the prodigal child makes a serendip soiree
deep ln December
as thousand somnolent horsemen rise
raring to cross the rubicon
and tear the dark grey mist asunder
a behemoth from an alternate world

57. Reuben's colt

preening december dawn

a Reubens' alabaster colt, as it were,

vain & baroque

(one could'nt miss its presumptuous swagger)

its mane auburn & afire

spidery witch-hazel bristled

(in anticipation)

demure dogwood blushed shot-silk

and coy hibiscus swooned

at its profligate caper!

(they feigned indifference though)

the mist- a billowing miasma

that laid seige on the dreary night

amorphous & grey-

withdrew its servile tongues

and readily made way

for Reuben's alabaster colt

the december dawn- preening....

58. A dirge on a December morning

grey remorse written large

over a squalid december morning

seemingly clipped merry wings of my words-

words once supple, sensuous & even flirtatious

now famished, brooding yet smitten

here it's not the promised land

flowing with milk & honey

it's rather a barren land where soul-mates wearing masks

walk past speaking of curious cases

of feigned equipoise and profligate words

wring & rend weary hearts-

disembodied spirits, they prowl

desolate savannah of mute longings

and gossamer flakes of purple angst

writhe in an unprecedented requiem

59. The pinchtail's dream

ebony silence
remorseless, cold & viscid
maim the conifers-
in melancohly servitude they sigh!
that perhaps the pinchtails will have
already taken flight
across seven seas
their tiny wings made strong & resilient
by the ruthless tundra
dreaming of a mysterious faraway wonderland
and beryl warmth of an amazing nest
of celebration!....

60. Sweet desperado

old yellow moon and I reminisce
for the umpteenth time-
of sweet desperado
of shackles & rainbow denials
we wore with such elan!
of philia or eros
of our so pathetic selves
and the fascinating survival game!

61. The witness

just another of the myriad
deepening nights-
this; an ebony waif, smitten & pensive
with all the familiar trappings
you know,
so much so, it breeds contempt!
the delinquent clouds
the ever itinerant charmers
their hearts on the tether
with a thousand livid tales to tell
(that just can't wait to be told-
a mythical release, that!)
the conniving old pedestrian moon;
the cedar grove, its mysterious crypts
and of course, the renegade muse
the sacrilege of a mute witness
to the plunder of a promised land
of myrrh, aloe
and flowing with milk & honey
all familiar trappings, you know-
so much so it breeds contempt!

62. Serendip soiree

spring noontide
breaks languid time into gossamer surf
in a silent haunting monotone
and lulls through majestic dreamways
into serendip soirees-
of now derelict ramparts of fortresses
none dared conquer...
also, mahogany boughs & streams
that witnessed the fairest of them all
none dared claim
but me!

63. Rendezvous

lapis lazuli moments waft
under an alabaster swathe
of the wizened moon and the Orion
angels stand guard
the spheres conspire
the west wind catches its breath
at such maverick desperado
of inane heartaches
and dollops of iridescent ecstasy
suffuse the firmament
as I walk into the vortex of sacred time
and a pining April night fawns
on the terrafirma
I have a rendezvous light years afar.....
tonight!

.....

64. Wondrous sojourn

incorrigible
the insolent & a voyeur moon
like a scheming prurient waif
wove sheer magic-
and dripping silver glee
rose over the stunned cedars
of Burlowgunj
smitten & weak at the knees....
one'd rather
a kindred minstrel had set up
a nightly rendezvous
with the 'old, phlegmatic & jaundiced' moon-
a frivolous muse!
transfigured, you & i'd witness
a sacred consecration
and walk
sands of a very gravid continuum
to this irridescent moment
that stretched zillion light-years
and wonder at
ordained possibilities
(that'd withered maimed & famished)
emerge elfinesque
from a wondrous wormhole...
across a multiverse
set in immaculate relief &

fecund with myriad lifetimes
of epic tales of our love & hatred!

65. Thought anemones

wriggling thought anemones
unbidden and relentless-
implode into nebulous figments of worn times
a beryl sun here, dripping gold
on wallowing verdant meadows in mirth
or a topaz moon there
looking over the sanctum of the bamboo grove
or, say the genteel east wind
(a lone, lorn waif) heaving a rustling sigh
the beckoning contours of a very nubile Meghna
the jackfruit fragrance of a philia
the coral warmth of a magpie nest-
all these and more;
and of course improbable dexterity & ease
we scaled light-years
and plucked stars with!
nebulous figments of yellow'd times
we miserably failed to live!

66. Implosion

the wizened oak
the demure pastel sky
browbeaten and sullied into a tryst
of servitude as it were
witness enraptured
this silent implosion of a dawn
a paen
that soars in concentric peals
from the sacred crypts
of a grey continuum-
a shibboleth
intimidating & relentless, this leviathan
yet stunningly beautiful
the eye of a bewitching maelstrom

67. Syntropy moment

the mountains
bidden as it were
by a sorceress' covenant-
one'd rather primeval hymns
would have frozen
into monoliths
and an ebony silence of the womb
lacquered in stardust & beryl moon flakes
wailed in allegretto
of zillion heartaches & coral angst
that morphed into maimed conifers-
the sentinels in stupor!
a zero-sum syntropy moment
a bridge across light years,
this!

68. Fixation

this fixation
retreading derelict ramparts
of monochrome silence
of hapless moments in relief
of exalted loss!
this miserable fixation
with inordinate self-pity
of an insidious consumption
as green tongues of pain
would morph into tender stigmata
and the reluctant muse
sing a soulful dirge
one last time and
soar on golden wings
into an alternate sky

oh! this sweet fixation
this exalted loss!

69. In comic relief

mellow colors of senescence,
a dollop of yellow here, sepia there-
strokes of many hued words
set the winter fresco
in comic relief!
and betray painfully feigned pubescence
(one might say)
of the proverbial nymphet
from the surreal & implausible shores
(we nested once)
that would've stunned the lonely unassuming
jakaranda
(she'd rustle a sigh though)
we had better
courageously inhabit
such intimidating space
(of broken covenants, renegade muse...etc)
as thought brigands
surreptitiously entice smitten words
too eager
strokes of many hued words
set the winter fresco
in comic relief!

70. Not the vintage moon

it wasn't the vintage moon
with quintessential prurience
(and the enigmatic charmer that he ever is)
labored up from behind
the sleepy mountain hamlet
and it wasn't like
the enraptured cedars & pines
were going weak at the knees
or the smitten hearts
of the luscious napier were agog in anticipation
or as if the moon- struck village belle
from the riverine plain
were wide awake & shifting in bed
for her boatman
long gone into a foreign land!
I would rather
the moon appeared ailing indeed
(since we had last met-
may be at the Mehrangarh fort or Noor-e-Darwaja
or was it the foot of Chingmeirong at Imphal valley?)
like someone that bleeds insidiously
to a sickly pallor

shorn of spunk & chutzpah
the mate failed to weave
its mesmeric spell on Titian's maenads

or Rembrandt's horses
(as is its wont)
and rouse them to an immaculate resurrection.

71. The 'six-pence' moon

for once
take my word, the nubile evening
(an eager wench as it were)
melted into sheer philia–
an immaculate senescence, this!
I reckon
it'd merrily die a mahogany death
and into a cold, preternatural night

a 'six pence' moon
(incorrigible voyeur that it is)
bristled at this rite of passage
as rainbow denial morphed
into monochrome benediction
and a thousand billowing tongues
of zircon silence rose
from dark crypts of this rhapsody
(of the dying evening in rapture)
and set the moment afire!
the solitary raven winging its way home
the curious oak grove
bullet wood & myrtle
and the profligate northwind
watched in awe
this syntropy moment of epiphany
that stretched light-years

72. Easy conviction

easy conviction
like soft velvet bosom of a magpie
impels
and tames rainbow rings of denial -
trepidations like sly vixen
that ran amok
hymns of atonement rise
as an offering -
the zircon fire
of the sacred travesty of passion & ennui
of lmprobable engagements
of ignominy & defeat
of lonely dreary sojourns & weariness
of the bizarre & the chequered
from the derelict ramparts
of a forsaken Kingdom

73. The mist

unassuming worn moments
that called time long ago
rose like a mist
from mysterious crypts of oblivion
and morphed light-years into a brilliant alternate sky
(we nested once upon a time) and
was perhaps the most azure
the itinerant geese too appeared
winging their way relentless to an eager savanna
nubile fields of poppy, corn & mustard-
filial glee welling up in their hearts
just the way it was
only the other day (as it were)
and of course
the coy lavender & effete hibiscus
the brazen magnolia and the wily cedar
all held their breath & braced against a frivolous northerly
with serrated teeth!
Unassuming worn moments
that called time long ago
rose like a mist.

74. Swarovski moment

it was just that

the scheme of things had to unfold

as bidden

those Swarovski moments-

bespoke and eminently fleeting,

yet

intense and seminal !

and , may be we even made it

to that zero-sum syntropy

of a tiffany blue oblivion

for an infinitesimal while

shall serenade that moment of epiphany

that profound revelation

as we run amok

on manicured pretenses & chamois facades

into that elusive baptism of truth

Mephestopheles of course stoods guard

with the entropy wand in hand

75. Zeitgeist

a preternatural animus
the silence held its breath
as one (a voyeur) watched this zeitgeist in glee
eager profligate words
merrily bleeding to their nemesis
and dying into momentous truth-
implausible smithy , this
at once zero-sum & myriad!
hence the solitude at the moment
was a thousand billowing tongues
rising from dark crypts of a zircon silence
viscid, cold & intimidating-
or instead a moon-struck prairie wolf's predicament
it was or say the milky way
musing a hymn braced itself bated
lest it broke into starry smithereens
and fell, simmering confetti these
drenched a Rembrandt's solitary horse
frolicking in an improbable Savannah
as a senescent evening deepened
into a mahogany night

76. Resolution

a scheming feline
its footfall servile & intimidating-
this balmy viscid dusk
might vicariously sweet- talk us
into a lurid mire of censure
self-pity & preservation
(like it has always done)
prod us to our knees
in abject defeat, cowardice
and rigmarole of convenience
I'd rather
we resolutely walk
defiantly oblivious of the encrypted time
and its foibles
to that unqualified syntropy moment
a primordium fecund with the infinite!

77. As usual

conniving prurience
of early autumn
and ribald scent of yellow'd times
shall browbeat us
stoke embers of rainbow denial
this evening too (as usual)
I'd rather we take a sabbatical
from this imminently predictable convenience
of veiled decay
rather call time
at that implausible & alternate shore
where we'd merely watch
restive hedonist words feed off
incarcerated nuances of time
vulturine, and morph into enigmas
of philia or eros
at once rustic mellow
feral , intense....

78. A saffron evening

this saffron evening
we talked of the boat-woman's wondrous trove
of fragrant myrrh & zircon
of potions & charms
we talked of the alleyways narrow & dark
the spectre of the witches on the tamarind tree
we talked of the cleft-lipp'd 'fakir' in red
how he'd say those sacred but silent words of his
and blow a sharp whiff of smelly air on our face
and exorcise the demons out of us!

79. Shrieking contrasts

a predicament lurks
as a billowimg silence mushrooms
into shreiking constructs in relief
the wizened oak, maimed mountains
& the last of the ravens winging its
way home, the deepening clouds
like conspiring brigands raring to strike-
they all seem to know
the encrypted secret!
a carnival of shreiking contrasts-
these; the intense gaze that set the dying
spring twilight afire on NH 39
the amazing chiaroscuro of despair & hope
at Noor-e- Darwaja or the stunning intaglio
of maverick engagements & foibles
in a somnolent Imphal valley
they all seem to know
the encrypted secret!

80. Pretense

it's onerous
carrying this stake of veiled pretense
that this bonhomie is all very right
it's just fine to exchange pleasantries
spin brocaded yarns of tinsel rhetoric
or engage Eliotesque with the weather
instead
this mid summer noon conspires
and impels I dare the forbidden Charybdis
the dark recesses
and ingots of incarcerating pain
that belie we nested in the lilac warmth
of revelation and glory
light years away
it's onerous
carrying this stake of veiled pretense

81. Beautiful nemesis

beige thought foxes prowl
jejune dreamscape
and tinsel sheer heartaches bleed
dollops of purple angst
feel tempted
to walk on razor's edge
to take beautiful nemesis by the jugular
to ride on the pegasus by the zephyr
once again!

82. A deepening quiet

its benediction, you know
sheer stroking with words
the canvas of the deepening quiet-
winged frolicking words, these
(that I shall engage, as usual)

shall cast, mould & chisel
truant words-eager & supple
into sentient vehicles to soar
and revisit once more the wanton hours
now frozen in another time
flaming green tendrils of passion & despair
feral & intense;
of thousand lusting tongues
afire with a zircon consumption!
the deepening quiet submits
to sheer wordstrokes-
it's benediction

83. But me!

spring noontide
breaks the languid time
into gossamer surf
in a silent, haunting monotone
and lulls through majestic dreamways
into serendip soirees
of now derelict ramparts of fortresses
none dared conquer
also, mahogany boughs & streams
that witnessed the fairest of them all
none dared claim
but me!

84. Spring saga

the golden oriole
bucolic dreams in its kohl eyes
green warmth of polynesian islands under its wings
and the petunias
connive & revel
in a riot of colored glee
springtide wells up
and sapphire tongues of bliss
light a rainbow implosion afire
in weary souls, miserable deluded souls
weaving tender bleeding yarns
of happiness - a scheming wench
for a tomorrow that never ever comes!

85. Not the vintage one

it wasn't the vintage moon
with quintessential prurience-
and the enigmatic charmer that he ever is
laboured up from behind the sleepy mountain hamlet
and it wasn't like
the enraptured cedars & pines were going weak at the knees
or the smitten hearts of the luscious napier
were agog in anticipation
or the moon- struck village belle from riverine plains
would be wide awake & shifting in bed
for her boatman long gone into a foreign land!
I would rather the moon appeared ailing indeed
(since we had last met
may be at the Mehrangarh fort or Noor-e-Darwaja
or was it the foot of Chingmeirong at Imphal valley?)
like someone that'd 've bled insidiously to a deathly pallor!
instead
shorn of spunk & chutzpah
the mate failed to weave its mesmeric spell
on Titian's maenads or Rembrandt's horses,
as is its wont,
to an immaculate resurrection

Mystique Of The Wily Troubadour

mystique of the wily troubadour

serenading peals from his tambourine

in concentric whorls reverberated & spun

> *an enchanting disquiet*

as the rapt morning listened to his travelogue

> *a wayfarer's tale*

> *from across bays & straits*

> *a tagoresque mien-*

> *this canvas of cascading rains*

eager profligate words couldn't wait to embellish

in wanton mirth!

and paint this séance a thousand hues

fleeting murals of moments of epiphany-

as maimed words rent their hearts

> *and bled*

> *the tambourine man danced away-*

> *mystique of the wily troubadour*